Richard Watson Gilder

The Poet and His Master, and Other Poems

Richard Watson Gilder

The Poet and His Master, and Other Poems

ISBN/EAN: 9783744772235

Printed in Europe, USA, Canada, Australia, Japan

Cover: Foto ©Thomas Meinert / pixelio.de

More available books at **www.hansebooks.com**

THE POET AND HIS MASTER,

AND OTHER POEMS.

I

THE POET AND HIS MASTER

AND OTHER POEMS,

BY

RICHARD WATSON GILDER,

AUTHOR OF "THE NEW DAY."

NEW-YORK:

CHARLES SCRIBNER'S SONS.

1878.

Press of
FRANCIS HART & CO.

CONTENTS.

Page.

ODE.

"I am the Spirit of the Morning Sea"............... 9

A SONG OF EARLY SUMMER.................... 14

A MIDSUMMER SONG......................... 16

"ON THE WILD ROSE TREE".................... 18

A SONG OF EARLY AUTUMN.................... 19

THE POET'S PROTEST......................... 21

WANTED, A THEME.......................... 22

"A WORD SAID IN THE DARK"................. 23

THE SONNET............................... 24

LONGFELLOW'S "BOOK OF SONNETS".......... 25

ESSIPOFF................................... 26

TO MODJESKA.............................. 27

THE DRAMA............................... 28

DECORATION DAY.......................... 31

"THE EVENING STAR"....................... 33

MORNING AND NIGHT....................... 34

6 *CONTENTS.*

Page.

A Woman's Thought...................35

"Reform"......37

For an Album. 39

Cost 41

The Homestead.................42

The White and the Red Rose...........44

Keats 47

"Call Me not Dead"...................48

A Thought..................49

Cradle Song..... 50

"Beyond the Branches of the Pine"..........51

Love and Death.

    I. "Now who can take from us what we have known".52

    II. "We know not where they tarry who have died"..53

"Back from the Darkness to the Light Again" 54

"When Love Dawned"...................55

The Poet's Fame...................56

The Poet and His Master. 63

ODE.

ODE.

I AM the spirit of the morning sea;
I am the awakening and the glad surprise;
I fill the skies
With laughter and with light.
Not tears, but jollity
At birth of day brim the strong man-child's eyes.
Behold the white
Wide three-fold beams that from the hidden sun
Rise swift and far,—
One where Orion keeps
His arméd watch, and one
That to the midmost starry heaven upleaps;
The third blots out the firm-fixed Northern Star.

2

I am the wind that shakes the glittering wave,
Hurries the snowy spume along the shore
And dies at last in some far-murmuring cave.
My voice thou hearest in the breaker's roar—
That sound which never failed since time began
And first around the world the shining tumult ran.

II.

I light the sea and wake the sleeping land.
My footsteps on the hills make music, and my hand
Plays like a harper's on the wind-swept pines.

With the wind and the day
I follow round the world—away! away!
Wide over lake and plain my sunlight shines,
And every wave and every blade of grass
Doth know me as I pass,
And me the western-sloping mountains know, and me
The far-off, golden sea.

O sea, whereon the passing sun doth lie!—
O man, who watchest by that golden sea!

Weep not,—Oh weep not thou, but lift thine eye
And see me glorious in the sunset sky!

III.

I love not the night
Save when the stars are bright,
Or when the moon
Fills the white air with silence like a tune.
Yea, even the night is mine
When Northern Lights outshine,
And the wild heavens throb in ecstasy divine;—
Yea, mine deep midnight, though the black sky lowers,
When the sea burns white and breaks on the shore
    in starry showers.

IV.

I am the laughter of the new-born child
On whose soft-breathing sleep an angel smiled.
And I all sweet first things that are:
First songs of birds, not perfect as at last—
Broken and incomplete—
But sweet, oh, sweet!

And I the first faint glimmer of a star
To the wrecked ship, that tells the storm is past;
The first keen smells and stirrings of the Spring;
First snow-flakes, and first May-flowers after snow;
The silver glow
Of the new moon's ethereal ring;
The song the morning stars together made,
And the first kiss of lovers under the first June shade.

v.

My sword is quick, my arm is strong to smite
In the dread joy and fury of the fight.
I am with those who win, not those who fly;
With those who live I am, not those who die.

Who die? Nay—nay—that word
Where I am is unheard;
For I am the spirit of youth that can not change,
Nor cease, nor suffer woe;
And I am the spirit of beauty that doth range
Through natural forms and motions, and each show
Of outward loveliness. With me have birth

All gentleness and joy in all the earth.
Raphael knew me, and showed the world my face;
Me Homer knew, and all the singing race,—
For I am the spirit of light, and life, and mirth.

A SONG OF EARLY SUMMER.

NOT yet the orchard lifted
  Its cloudy bloom to the sky,
Nor through the dim twilight drifted
  The whip-poor-will's low cry;

The gray rock had not made
  Of the vine its glistening kirtle;
  The purple bells of the myrtle
Shook not in the locust shade.

Ere, awake in the darkling night
  Is heard in the chimney-hollow
  The boom and whir of the swallow
And the twitter that follows the flight;

Before the foamy whitening
  Of the water below the mill;
Ere yet the summer lightning
  Shone red at the edge of the hill—

In the time of sun and showers,
  Of skies half-black, half-clear ;
'Twixt melting snows and flowers ;
  At the poise of the flying year;

When woods flushed pink and yellow
  In dreams of leafy June ;
And days were keen or mellow
  Like tones in a changing tune —

Before the birds had broken
  Forth in their song divine,
Oh ! then the word was spoken
  That made my darling mine.

A MIDSUMMER SONG.

Oʜ, father's gone to market-town, he was up before
the day,

And Jamie's after robins, and the man is making
hay,

And whistling down the hollow goes the boy that
minds the mill,

While mother from the kitchen-door is calling with
a will,

" Polly! — Polly! — The cows are in the corn!
Oh, where's Polly?"

From all the misty morning air there comes a sum-
mer sound,—

A murmur as of waters from skies, and trees and
ground.

The birds they sing upon the wing, the pigeons bill
and coo,

And over hill and hollow rings again the loud halloo:

" Polly! — Polly! — The cows are in the corn!
Oh, where's Polly?"

Above the trees the honey-bees swarm by with buzz
    and boom,
And in the field and garden a thousand blossoms
    bloom.
Within the farmer's meadow a brown-eyed daisy blows,
And down at the edge of the hollow a red and
    thorny rose.
      But Polly! — Polly! — The cows are in the corn!
      Oh, where 's Polly?

How strange at such a time of day the mill should
    stop its clatter!
The farmer's wife is listening now and wonders what 's
    the matter.
Oh, wild the birds are singing in the wood and on
    the hill,
While whistling up the hollow goes the boy that
    minds the mill.
      But Polly! — Polly! —The cows are in the corn!
      Oh, where 's Polly?

3

"ON THE WILD ROSE TREE."

On the wild rose tree
Many buds there be,
Yet each sunny hour
Hath but one perfect flower.

Thou who wouldst be wise
Open wide thine eyes,—
In each sunny hour
Pluck the one perfect flower!

A SONG OF EARLY AUTUMN.

WHEN late in summer the streams run yellow,
  Burst the bridges and spread into bays;
When berries are black and peaches are mellow,
  And hills are hidden by rainy haze;

When the golden-rod is golden still,
  But the heart of the sun-flower is darker and sadder;
When the corn is in stacks on the slope of the hill,
  And slides o'er the path the stripéd adder.

When butterflies flutter from clover to thicket,
  Or wave their wings on the drooping leaf;
When the breeze comes shrill with the call of the
    cricket —
  Grasshoppers' rasp, and rustle of sheaf.

When high in the field the fern-leaves wrinkle,
  And brown is the grass where the mowers have
    mown;
When low in the meadow the cow-bells tinkle,
  And small brooks crinkle o'er stock and stone.

When heavy and hollow the robin's whistle,
  And shadows are deep in the heat of noon;
When the air is white with the down o' the thistle,
  And the sky is red with the harvest moon;

O then be chary, young Robert and Mary,
  No time let slip, not a moment wait!
    If the fiddle would play it must stop its tuning,
    And they who would wed must be done with
      their mooning.
Let the churn rattle, see well to the cattle,
  And pile the wood by the barn-yard gate!

THE POET'S PROTEST.

O MAN with your rule and measure,
  Your tests and analyses!
You may take your empty pleasure,
  May kill the pine, if you please;
You may count the rings and the seasons,
  May hold the sap to the sun,
You may guess at the ways and the reasons
  Till your little day is done.

But for me the golden crest
  That shakes in the wind and launches
Its spear toward the reddening West!
  For me the bough and the breeze,
The sap unseen, and the glint
  Of light on the dew-wet branches,—
The hiding shadows, the hint
  Of the soul of mysteries.

You may sound the sources of life,
    And prate of its aim and scope;
You may search with your chilly knife
    Through the broken heart of hope.
But for me the love-sweet breath,
    And the warm, white bosom heaving,
And never a thought of death,
    And only the bliss of living.

" GIVE me a theme," the little poet cried,
    " And I will do my part."
" 'T is not a theme you need," the world replied;
    " You need a heart."

" A WORD SAID IN THE DARK."

A WORD said in the dark
And hands pressed, for a token;
" Now, little maiden, mark
The word that you have spoken;
Be not your promise broken ! "

His lips upon her cheek
Felt tears among their kisses;
" O pardon I bespeak
If for my doubting this is !
Now all my doubting ceases."

THE SONNET.

(IN ANSWER TO A QUESTION.)

WHAT is a sonnet? 'T is the pearly shell
    That murmurs of the far-off murmuring sea;
    A precious jewel carved most curiously;
    It is a little picture painted well.
What is a sonnet? 'T is the tear that fell
    From a great poet's hidden ecstasy;
    A two-edged sword, a star, a song—ah me!
    Sometimes a heavy-tolling funeral bell.
This was the flame that shook with Dante's breath;
    The solemn organ whereon Milton played,
    And the clear glass where Shakespeare's shadow falls:
A sea this is—beware who ventureth!
    For like a fjord the narrow floor is laid
    Deep as mid-ocean to the sheer mountain walls.

LONGFELLOW'S "BOOK OF SONNETS."

Last Sunday evening as I wandered down
  The central highway of this swarming place,
  I felt a pleasant stillness — not a trace
  Of Saturday's wild turmoil in the town :
Then as a gentle breeze just stirs a gown,
  Yet almost motionless, or as the face
  Of silence smiles, I heard the chimes of " Grace"
  Sound murmuring through the autumn evening's
    brown.
To-day, again, I passed along Broadway
  In the fierce tumult and mid-noise of noon,
  While under my feet the solid pavement shook;
When lo ! it seemed that bells began to play
  Upon a Sabbath eve a silver tune,—
  For as I walked I read the poet's book.

4

ESSIPOFF.

I.

WHAT is her playing like?
I ask—while dreaming here under her music's power.
'T is like the leaves of the dark passion-flower
Which grows on a strong vine whose roots, oh deep
    they sink,
Deep in the ground, that flower's pure life to drink.

II.

What is her playing like?
'T is like a bird
Who, singing in a wild wood, never knows
That its lone melody is heard
By wandering mortal, who forgets his heavy woes.

TO MODJESKA.

THERE are four sisters known to mortals well,
 Whose names are Joy and Sorrow, Death and Love:
 This last it was who did my footsteps move
 To where the other deep-eyed sisters dwell.
To-night, or ere yon painted curtain fell,
 These, one by one, before my eyes did rove
 Through the brave mimic world that Shakspere wove.
 Lady! thy art, thy passion were the spell
That held me, and still holds; for thou dost show,
 With those most high each in his sovereign art,—
 Shakspere supreme, Beethoven and Angelo,—
Great art and passion are one. Thine too the part
 To prove, that still for him the laurels grow
 Who reaches through the mind to pluck the heart.

THE DRAMA.

(FROM THE POLISH.)

I sat in the crowded theater. The first notes of the orchestra wandered in the air; then the full harmony burst forth; then ceased.

The conductor, secretly pleased with the loud applause, waited a moment, then played again; but as he struck upon his desk for the third time, the bell sounded, the just-beginning tones of the wind-instruments and the violins hushed suddenly, and the curtain was rolled to the ceiling.

Then appeared to me a wonderful vision, which still clings to my mind, and shall not soon be forgotten by me.

For know that I am one who loves all things beautiful. Did you find the figure of a man lying solitary upon the wind-fashioned hills of sand, watching the large sun rise from the ocean? That was I.

It was I who, lonely, walked at evening through the woods of autumn, beholding the sun's level light strike through the unfallen red and yellow leaves;

Whose heart trembled when he saw the fire that rapidly consumed the dead leaves lying upon the hillside, and spread a robe of black that throbbed with crimson jewels under the wind of the rushing flame.

Know, also, that the august forms wrought in marble by the ancient sculptors have power upon me; also the imaginative works of the incomparable painters; and that the voices of the early poets are modern and familiar to me.

What vision was it, then, that I beheld; what art was it that made my heart tremble and filled me with joy that was like pain?

Was it the art of the poet; was it of a truth poetry made visible in human attitudes and motions and many changing tones?

Was it the art of the painter—which Raphael knew so well when he created those most gracious shapes that yet live on the walls of the Vatican?

Or was it the severe and marvelous art of the sculptor, in which antique Phidias excelled, and which Michael Angelo indued with new and mighty power?

Or, haply, it was that enchanting myth, made real before our eyes,—of the insensate marble warmed to life beneath the passionate gaze of the sculptor!

No, no; it was not this miracle, of which the bards have so often sung; nor was it the art of the poet, nor of the painter, nor of the musician (though often I thought of music), nor of the sculptor.   It was none of these that moved my heart, and the hearts of all who beheld,—

It was the ancient and noble art of the drama,—the oldest of all the arts, because the most natural, that one which is indeed informed of all the others,—and she who was the mistress of it was none other than the divine Modjeska.

DECORATION DAY.

I.

She saw the bayonets flashing in the sun,
The flags that proudly waved, the bands, the bugles
    calling ;
She saw the tattered banners falling
About the broken staffs, as one by one
The remnant of the mighty army passed ;
And at the last
Flowers for the graves of those whose fight was done.

II.

She heard the tramping of ten thousand feet
As the long line swept round the crowded square ;
She heard the incessant hum
That filled the warm and blossom-scented air,—
The shrilling fife, the roll and throb of drum,

The happy laugh, the cheer.— Oh glorious and meet
To honor thus the dead,
Who chose the better part
And for their country bled!
—The dead! Great God! she stood there in the street,
Living, yet dead in soul and mind and heart—
While far away
His grave was decked with flowers by strangers'
    hands to-day.

NEW-YORK, May 30, 1877.

"THE EVENING STAR."

THE evening star trembles and hides from him
  Who fain would hold it with imperious stare;
  Yet, to the averted eye, lo! unaware
  It shines serene, no longer shy and dim.
Oh, slow and sweet, its chalice to the brim
  Fills the leaf-shadowed grape with rich and rare
  Cool sunshine, caught from the white circling air!
  Home from his journey to the round world's rim—
Through lonely lands, through cloudy seas and vext—
  At last the Holy Grail met Launfal's sight.
  So when my friend lost him who was her next
Of soul,—life of her life,—all day the fight
  Raged with a dumb and pitiless God. Perplexed
  She slept. Heaven sent its comfort in the night.

MORNING AND NIGHT.

THE mountain that the morn doth kiss
   Glad greets its shining neighbor :
Lord ! heed the homage of our bliss,—
   The incense of our labor.

Now the long shadows eastward creep,
   The golden sun is setting :
Take, Lord ! the worship of our sleep,—
   The praise of our forgetting.

A WOMAN'S THOUGHT.

I am a woman—therefore I may not
Call to him, cry to him,
Fly to him,
Bid him delay not!

And when he comes to me, I must sit quiet:
Still as a stone,—
All silent and cold.
If my heart riot—
Crush and defy it!
Should I grow bold—
Say one dear thing to him,
All my life fling to him,
Cling to him—
What to atone
Is enough for my sinning!

This were the cost to me,
This were my winning —
That he were lost to me.

Not as a lover
At last if he part from me,
Tearing my heart from me, —
Hurt beyond cure, —
Calm and demure
Then must I hold me, —
In myself fold me, —
Lest he discover;
Showing no sign to him
By look of mine to him
What he has been to me, —
How my heart yearns to him,
Follows him, turns to him,
Prays him to love me.

Pity me, lean to me,
Thou God above me!

" REFORM."

I.

Oh, how shall I help to right the world that is
 going wrong !
And what can I do to hurry the promised time of
 peace !
The day of work is short and the night of sleep is
 long;
And whether to pray or preach, or whether to sing
 a song,
To plow in my neighbor's field, or to seek the golden
 fleece,
Or to sit with my hands in my lap, and wish that
 sin would cease !

II.

I think, sometimes, it were best just to let the Lord
 alone;
I am sure some people forget He was here before
 they came;

Though they say it is all for His glory, 't is a good
    deal more for their own,
That they peddle their petty schemes, and blate and
    babble and groan.
I sometimes think it were best, and I were little to
    blame,
Should I sit with my hands in my lap, in my face
    a crimson shame.

FOR AN ALBUM.

(TO BE READ ONE HUNDRED YEARS AFTER.)

A century's summer breezes shook
   The maple shadows on the grass
Since she who owned this ancient book
   From the green world to heaven did pass.

Beside a northern lake she grew,
   A wild-flower on its craggy walls;
Her eyes were mingled gray and blue,
   Like waves where summer sunlight falls.

Cheerful her hours from morn to close
   Of day, no work nor prayer forgot:
Yet who of woman born but knows
   The sorrows of our mortal lot!

And she too suffered, though the wound
   Was hidden from the general gaze,

And most from those who thus had found
    An added burden to their days.

She had no special grace, nor art;
    Her riches not in banks were kept:
Her treasure was a gentle heart,
    Her skill to comfort those who wept.

Not without foes her days were passed,
    For quick her burning scorn was fanned.
Her friends were many—least and last,
    A poet from a distant land.

COST.

BECAUSE Heaven's cost is Hell, and perfect joy
   Hurts as hurts sorrow; and because we win
   No boon of grace without the cost of sin,
   Or suffering born of sin; because the alloy
Of blood but makes the bliss of victory brighter;
   Because true worth hath its sure proof herein—
   That it should be reproached, and called akin
   To evil things—black making white the whiter:
Because no cost seems great near this—that He
   Should pay the ransom wherewith we were priced;
   And none could name a mightier infamy
Than that a God was spit upon—enticed
   By those he came to save, to the damnéd tree—
   Therefore I know that Christ indeed is Christ.

6

THE HOMESTEAD.

I.

HERE stays the house, here stay the self-same places,
Here the white lilacs and the buttonwoods;
Here are the pine-groves, there the river-floods,
And there the threading brook that interlaces
Green meadow-bank with meadow-bank the same.
The melancholy nightly chorus came
Long, long ago from the same pool, and yonder
Stark poplars lift in the same twilight air
Their ancient shadows: nearer still. and fonder,
The black-heart cherry-tree's gaunt branches bare
Rasp on the same old window where I ponder.

II.

And we, the only living, only pass;
We come and go, whither and whence we know not:
From birth to bound the same house keeps, alas!
New lives as gently as the old; there show not
Among the haunts that each had thought his own
The changes parting brings to human faces.
The black-heart there, that heard my earliest moan,
And yet shall hear my last, like all these places
I love so well, unloving lives from child
To child; from morning joy to evening sorrow—
Untouched by joy, by anguish undefiled:
All one the generations gone, and new;
All one dark yesterday and bright to-morrow;
To the old trees insensate sympathy
All one the morning and the evening dew—
My long-forgotten ancestor and I.

THE WHITE AND THE RED ROSE.

I.

In Heaven's happy bowers
There blossom two flowers,
One with fiery glow
And one as white as snow;
While lo! before them stands,
With pale and trembling hands,
A spirit who must choose
One, and one refuse.

II.

Oh, tell me of these flowers
That bloom in heavenly bowers,
One with fiery glow,
And one as white as snow!
And tell me who is this
In Heaven's holy bliss
Who trembles and cries
Like a mortal that dies!

III.

These blossoms two
Wet with heavenly dew —
The Gentle Heart is one,
And one is Beauty's own;
And the spirit here that stands
With pale and trembling hands —
Before to-morrow's morn
Will be a child new-born,
Will be a mortal maiden
With earthly sorrows laden;
But of these shining flowers
That bloom in heavenly bowers,
To-day she still may choose
One, and one refuse.

IV.

Will she pluck the crimson flower
And win Beauty's dower?
Will she choose the better part

And gain the Gentle Heart?
Awhile she weeping waits
Within those pearly gates —
Alas! the mortal maiden
With earthly sorrow laden:
Her tears afresh they start,
She has chosen the Gentle Heart.

V.

And now the spirit goes,
In her breast the snow-white rose.
When hark! a voice that calls
Within the garden walls:
"Thou didst choose the better part,
Thou hast won the Gentle Heart —
Lo, now to thee is given
The red rose of Heaven."

KEATS.

Touch not with dark regret his perfect fame,
    Sighing, " Had he but lived he had done so ; "
    Or, " Were his heart not eaten out with woe
    John Keats had won a prouder, mightier name ! "
Take him for what he was and did — nor blame
    Blind fate for all he suffered. Thou shouldst know
    Souls such as his escape no mortal blow —
    No agony of joy, or sorrow, or shame !
" Whose name was writ in water ! " What large laughter
    Among the immortals when that word was brought !
    Then when his fiery spirit rose flaming after
High toward the topmost heaven of heavens up-caught !
    " All hail ! our younger brother ! " Shakespeare said,
    And Dante nodded his imperial head.

"CALL ME NOT DEAD."

CALL me not dead when I, indeed, have gone
   Into the company of the ever living
   High and most glorious poets! Let thanksgiving
Rather be made. Say—"He at last hath won
Release and rest, converse supreme and wise,
   Music and song and light of immortal faces:
   To-day, perhaps, wandering in starry places,
He hath met Keats, and known him by his eyes.
To-morrow (who can say) Shakespeare may pass,—
   And our lost friend just catch one syllable
   Of that three-centuried wit that kept so well,—
Or Milton,—or Dante, looking on the grass
   Thinking of Beatrice, and listening still
   To chanted hymns that sound from the heavenly hill."

A THOUGHT.

ONCE, looking from a window on a land
That lay in silence underneath the sun:
A land of broad, green meadows, through which poured
Two rivers, slowly widening to the sea,—
Thus, as I looked, I know not how or whence,
Was borne into my unexpectant soul
That thought, late learned by anxious-witted man,
The infinite patience of the Eternal Mind.

CRADLE SONG.

In the embers shining bright
A garden grows for thy delight,
With roses yellow, red, and white.

But, O my child, beware, beware!
Touch not the roses growing there,
For every rose a thorn doth bear.

"BEYOND THE BRANCHES OF THE PINE."

BEYOND the branches óf the pine
The golden sun no more doth shine,
   But still the solemn after-glow
Floods the deep heavens with light divine.

The night-wind stirs the corn-field near—
The gray moon turns to silver clear,
   And one by one the glimmering stars
In the blue dome of heaven appear.

Now do the mighty hosts of light
Across the darkness take their flight,—
   They rise above the eastern hill
And silent journey through the night.

And there beneath the starry zone
In the deep, narrow grave, alone,
   Rests all that mortal was of her,
The purest spirit I have known.

LOVE AND DEATH.

I.

Now who can take from us what we have known —
  We that have looked into each other's eyes?
  Though sudden night should blacken all the skies,
  The day is ours, and what the day has shown.
What we have seen and been, hath not this grown
  Part of our very selves? We, made love-wise,
  What power shall slay our living memories,
  And who shall take from us what is our own?
So, when a shade of the last parting fell,
  This thought gave peace, as he deep comfort hath
  Who, thirsting, drinks cool waters from a well.
But soon I felt more near the fatal breath
  Of the body bodiless, the invisible
  Maker of visible woe,—I looked on Death.

II.

We know not where they tarry who have died;
  The gate wherein they entered is made fast:
  No living mortal hath seen one who passed
  Hither, from out that darkness deep and wide.
We lean on Faith; and some less wise have cried,
  " Behold the butterfly, the seed that 's cast!"
  Vain hopes that fall like flowers before the blast!
  What man can look on Death unterrified?
None, none, save those who love! They are a part
  Of all that lives beneath the summer sky;
  With the world's living soul their souls are one:
Nor shall they in vast nature be undone
  And lost in the general life. Each separate heart
  Shall live, and find its own, and never die.

"BACK FROM THE DARKNESS TO THE
LIGHT AGAIN."

"Back from the darkness to the light again!"—
Not from the darkness, Love, for hadst thou lain
Within the shadowy portal of the tomb,
Thy light had warmed the darkness into bloom.

"WHEN LOVE DAWNED."

WHEN love dawned on that world which is my mind,
  Then did the outer world wherein I went
  Suffer a sudden strange transfigurement—
  It was as if new sight were given the blind.
Then where the shore to the wide sea inclined
  I watched with new eyes the new sun's ascent:
  My heart was stirred within me as I leant
  And listened to a voice in every wind.
O purple sea! O joy beyond control!
  O land of love and youth! O happy throng!
  Were ye then real, or did ye only seem?
Dear is that morning twilight of the soul.—
  The mystery, and the waking voice of song,—
  For now I know it was not all a dream.

THE POET'S FAME.

Many the songs of power the poet wrought
To shake the hearts of men. Yea, he had caught
The inarticulate and murmuring sound
That comes at midnight from the darkened ground
When the earth sleeps ; for this he framed a word
Of human speech, and hearts were strangely stirred
That listened. And for him the evening dew
Fell with a sound of music, and the blue
Of the deep, starry sky he had the art
To put in language that did seem a part
Of the great scope and progeny of nature.
In woods, or waves, or winds, there was no creature
Mysterious to him. He was too wise
Either to fear, or follow, or despise
Whom men call Science,—for he knew full well
What she had told, or still might live to tell,
Was known to him before her very birth:

Yea, that there was no secret of the earth,
Nor of the waters under, nor the skies,
That had been hidden from the poet's eyes;
By him there was no ocean unexplored,
Nor any savage coast that had not roared
Its music in his ears.

He loved the town,—
Not less he loved the ever-deepening brown
Of summer twilights on the enchanted hills;
Where he might listen to the starts and thrills
Of birds that sang and rustled in the trees,
Or watch the footsteps of the wandering breeze
And the birds' shadows as they fluttered by
Or slowly wheeled across the unclouded sky.
All these were written on the poet's soul,—
But he knew, too, the utmost distant goal
Of the human mind. His fiery thought did run
To Time's beginnings, ere yon central sun
Had warmed to life the swarming broods of men.
In waking dreams, his many-visioned ken
Clutched the large, final destiny of things.

8

He heard the starry music, and the wings
Of beings unfelt by others thrilled the air
About him.　Yet the loud and angry blare
Of tempests found an echo in his verse,
And it was here that lovers did rehearse
The ditties they would sing when, not too soon,
Came the warm night,—shadows, and stars, and moon.

　　Who heard his songs were filled with noble rage,
And wars took fire from his prophetic page:
Most righteous wars, wherein, 'midst blood and tears,
The world rushed onward through a thousand years.
Nathless, he made the gentle sounds of peace
Heroic,—bade the nation's anger cease!
Bitter his songs of grief for those who fell—
And for all this the people loved him well.

　　They loved him well, and therefore, on a day,
They said, with one accord: " Behold how gray
Our poet's head hath grown!　Ere 't is too late
Come, let us crown him in our Hall of State:
Let the bells ring, give to the winds his praise,
And urge his fame to other lands and days!"

So was it done, and deep his joy therein.
But passing home at night, from out the din
Of the loud Hall, the poet, unaware,
Moved through a lonely and dim-lighted square—
There was the smell of lilacs in the air
And then the sudden singing of a bird,
Startled by his slow tread. What memory stirred
Within his brain he told not. Yet this night—
Still lingering when the eastern heavens were bright—
He wove a song of such immortal art
That there is not in all the world one heart—
One human heart unmoved by it. Long! long!
The laurel-crown has failed, but not that song
Born of the night and sorrow; and where he lies
At rest beneath the ever-shifting skies,
Age after age, from far-off lands they come,
Not without flowers, to seek the poet's tomb.

THE POET AND HIS MASTER.

THE POET AND HIS MASTER.

ONE day the poet's harp lay on the ground,
    Though from it rose a strange and trembling
      sound
What time the wind swept over with a moan,
Or, now and then, a faint and tinkling tone,
When a dead leaf fell shuddering from a tree
And shook the silent wires all tremulously;
And near it, solemn-eyed and woe-begone,
The poet sat: he did not weep or groan.

Then one drew nigh him who was robed in white:
It was the poet's master; he had given
To him that harp, once in a happy night

When every silver star that shone in heaven
Made music ne'er before was heard by mortal wight.
And thus the master spoke :

                    " Why is thy voice
Silent, O poet ?   Why upon the grass
Lies thy still harp ?   The fitful breezes pass
And touch the wires, but the skilled player's hand
Moves not upon them.   Poet,— wake !   Rejoice,
Sing and arouse the melancholy land."

" Master, forbear.   I may not sing to-day :
My nearest friend, the brother of my heart,
This day is stricken with sorrow, he must part
From her who loves him.   Can I sing, and play
Upon the joyous harp, and mock his woe ? "

" Alas, and hast thou then so soon forgot
The bond that with thy gift of song did go —
Severe as fate, fixed and unchangeable ?
Dost thou not know this is the poet's lot !
'Mid sounds of war — in halcyon times of peace —
To strike the ringing wire and not to cease :

In hours of general happiness to swell
The common joy; and when the people cry
With piteous voice loud to the pitiless sky,
'T is his to frame the universal prayer,
And breathe the balm of song upon the accurséd
    air ?"

"But 't is not, O my master, that I borrow
The robe of grief to deck my brother's sorrow,—
Mine eyes have seen beyond the veil of youth;
I know what Life is, have caught sight of Truth;
My heart is dead within me; a thick pall
Darkens the mid-day sun."

               "And dost thou call
This sorrow ? Call this knowledge? O thou blind
And ignorant! Know, then, thou yet shalt find,
Ere thy full days are numbered 'neath the sun,
Thou, in thy shallow youth, hadst but begun
To guess what knowledge is, what grief may be,
And all the infinite sum of human misery;
Shalt find for each rich drop of perfect good
Thou payest, at last, a threefold price in blood;   .

9

What is most noble in thee—every thought
Highest and best—crushed, spat upon, and brought
To an open shame; thy natural ignorance
Counted thy crime; the world all ruled by chance,
Save that the good most suffer; but above
These ills another,—cruel, monstrous, worse
Than all before,—thy pure and passionate love
Shall bring the old, immitigable curse."

"And thou who tell'st me this, dost bid me sing?"

" I bid thee sing, even though I have not told
All the deep flood of anguish shall be rolled
Across thy breast. Nor, Poet, shalt thou bring
From out those depths thy grief! Tell to the wind
Thy private woes, but not to human ear,
Save in the shape of comfort for thy kind.
But never hush thy song, dare not to cease
While life is thine. Haply, 'mid those who hear,
Thy music to one soul shall murmur peace,
Though for thyself it hath no power to cheer.

" Then shall thy still unbroken spirit grow
Strong in its suffering and more tender-wise ;
And as the drenched and thunder-shaken skies
Pass into golden sunset — thou shalt know
An end of calm, when evening breezes blow ;
And looking on thy life with vision fine
Shalt see the shadow of a hand divine."

www.ingramcontent.com/pod-product-compliance
Lightning Source LLC
Chambersburg PA
CBHW022022080426
42733CB00007B/685